· ♥ · ♥ · ♥ · ♥ · ♥ ·

I am the author of my own story, and I choose to write a narrative of empowerment and positivity. With each chapter, I craft a tale of resilience, growth, and boundless strength, where setbacks are merely stepping stones to success. My journey is a testament to the unwavering power of self-belief and the limitless potential that lies within me

• ♥ • ♥ • ♥ • ♥ • ♥ •

I am the architect of my destiny, shaping a life filled with purpose, love, and fulfillment. With each choice I make, I build a path to a future brimming with joy and success. I trust in my ability to create the life of my dreams.

I attract abundance and prosperity into my life effortlessly. The universe conspires in my favor, aligning circumstances and opportunities for my success. I am open to receiving the wealth and abundance that flow to me with ease.

As the butterfly gracefully emerges from its cocoon, I too embrace transformation with open arms. I am a symbol of beauty and resilience, just like the butterfly, and I am capable of incredible growth. With each flutter of my wings, I soar higher, radiating my inner light and inspiring others to embrace their own metamorphosis.

I am a fierce and resilient woman, capable of conquering any obstacle that stands in my way. With unwavering determination, I embrace challenges as opportunities for growth and success. My journey is a testament to the boundless strength that resides within me.

·♥·♥·♥·♥·♥·

I am a source of inspiration and support for other women on their journey to self-love and empowerment.   I lift up other women, reminding them of their inherent strength, resilience, and worthiness. I celebrate their victories, no matter how small, and provide a shoulder to lean on during moments of doubt

·♥·♥·♥·♥·♥·

My worth is not determined by my appearance; I am beautiful just as I am. The size of my stomach and hips does not define me or my value. I embrace my body's unique shape and celebrate its beauty in all its forms. I am a vessel of strength, kindness, and limitless potential. My true beauty radiates from the love and confidence I carry within.

I am confident in my abilities and trust myself to make the right decisions. Despite moments of doubt that may cross my path, I recognize them as mere ripples in the sea of my self-assuredness. I navigate through uncertainty with unwavering belief in my capabilities, emerging stronger and more resolute in my ability to steer the course of my life.

I am the embodiment of strength and resilience, overcoming obstacles with grace and determination. I trust in my ability to navigate life's twists and turns, emerging victorious with unwavering perseverance. My inner fortitude is unwavering.

I release the need for external validation and embrace the radiance of my true self. I am not defined by the judgments of others but by the love and acceptance I hold within. My image is a canvas of authenticity, and I paint it with confidence, knowing that I am uniquely beautiful.

We invite you to be part of our mission to spread positivity and empower women of all ages. 'Empowering Mandalas for Women and Teen Girls' is a heartfelt bonding collaboration between a mother and her 16-year-old daughter.
If you've found inspiration in our book or simply enjoyed coloring, please consider leaving an **Amazon review.**

Your words can help us reach more hearts and souls, nurturing the strength, grace, and resilience of women and girls everywhere. Together, let's inspire and uplift each other.

❦ · ❦ · ❦ · ❦ · ❦ · ❦

I am a force to be reckoned with, and I can achieve anything I set my mind to. My determination knows no bounds, and I approach challenges with unwavering courage. I am the architect of my own success, and my journey is a testament to the extraordinary strength that resides within me.

As a strong woman, I embrace my body's unique shape, knowing that it's a testament to my strength and life experiences. My hips, like the curves of a winding river, carry the stories of resilience and wisdom. I celebrate every inch of my body, for it reflects the journey of a powerful and empowered woman.

I am a beacon of confidence and self-assuredness, radiating positivity in every aspect of my life. I trust my intuition and make decisions with clarity and conviction. My choices are a reflection of my inner power and unwavering self-belief.

I possess the profound strength to nurture and create life, connecting deeply with the universe's rhythm; I embrace this gift with love and courage, a testament to my boundless capacity to bring forth and sustain the beauty of existence.

I celebrate my unique beauty and individuality, recognizing that true allure lies in authenticity. I am not defined by society's standards but by the love and acceptance I hold for myself. With each day, I grow stronger, more self-assured, and more deeply in love with the incredible woman I am becoming.

With each breath, I inhale confidence and exhale doubt. I trust in my abilities and acknowledge that I have the power to shape my destiny.

·♥·♥·♥·♥·♥·

I embrace my worthiness and stand tall in my authenticity. My voice is a beacon of empowerment, inspiring change and nurturing a world where all women are celebrated and supported.

I am a reservoir of strength, capable of achieving whatever I set my mind to. Each day, I grow stronger and more resilient, turning challenges into opportunities for growth.

My journey is filled with endless possibilities. Each step I take is a leap towards new adventures, exciting experiences, and fulfilling achievements.

I am the architect of my dreams, fearlessly shaping my destiny with purpose and passion. I radiate love, kindness, and grace, creating a life that reflects my inner power.

♥ · ♥ · ♥ · ♥ · ♥

I am my own guardian, fiercely protecting my peace and well-being with the strength of my resolve. In every moment, I choose actions that nurture and safeguard my spirit, standing strong in the face of adversity. My inner strength is my shield, ensuring that I remain resilient, balanced, and true to myself.

With each passing year, I embrace my journey of aging gracefully, seeing the beauty and wisdom that come with time. I celebrate the stories etched in every line, each a testament to a life richly lived and loved. In my heart and soul, I carry the elegance of experience, aging not just in years, but in depth and joy.

I embody the ability to nurture life, reflecting the vast, nurturing nature of the world; within me lies the incredible potential to foster, protect, and inspire, a role that seamlessly intertwines with the essence of womanhood and the cycle of life.

I carry my worth like a queen, crown held high and straight, unwavering and intrinsic. With my head held high, I embody self-assurance, and my inner confidence radiates outward, drawing others to my magnetic presence. I inspire positivity and empowerment wherever I go, navigating the world with grace and the poise of royalty.

· ♥ · ♥ · ♥ · ♥ · ♥ ·

I am a warrior in my own right, facing each day with courage and resilience; within me lies the strength of a thousand battles, and the wisdom of a peaceful heart. Like a true warrior, I forge my path with determination, embracing every experience as an opportunity to grow stronger and more fearless.

The mirror reflects only a moment in time, and how I look today doesn't define my worth or potential. I carry an inner light that radiates confidence, beauty, and strength, regardless of external appearances.

I am a champion of self-care, nurturing my physical, emotional, and mental well-being. I prioritize my health and happiness, recognizing that self-care is a vital foundation for a fulfilling life. With each self-loving act, I replenish my energy and inner strength.

Even on days when the sun hides and shadows fall, I rise with determination, knowing that each step forward brings me closer to my goals. With every challenge, I grow stronger, turning each obstacle into a stepping stone on my path to success.

· ♥ · ♥ · ♥ · ♥ · ♥ ·

I am complete and whole on my own, and my worth is not defined by my relationship status. I embrace my independence and self-love as the foundation of my happiness. Whether in a relationship or single, I am a strong and empowered individual.

I choose joy and positivity in every moment, becoming guarding my own happiness. I let go of external negativity, instead embracing gratitude, finding joy in life's simplest pleasures. My happiness is an inner light, shining brightly and guiding my way.

I am a lifelong learner, continuously expanding my knowledge and wisdom. I embrace challenges as opportunities to grow and evolve, and I am unafraid of venturing into the unknown. My quest for knowledge fuels my personal and professional growth.

♥ · ♥ · ♥ · ♥ · ♥

I am a source of inspiration and support for those around me, uplifting and empowering others on their journeys. My words and actions create a positive impact, igniting the flames of hope and motivation in the hearts of those I touch. Together, we rise and thrive, creating a world filled with love and possibility.

I am a beacon of light, radiating love and kindness to all I encounter. My compassion knows no bounds, and I extend understanding and support to those in need. Through acts of kindness, I create a ripple effect of love and positivity in the world.

·♥·♥·♥·♥·♥·

I am a source of inspiration and support for those around me, uplifting and empowering others on their journeys. My words and actions create a positive impact, igniting the flames of hope and motivation in the hearts of those I touch.

I am the essence of beauty and confidence, and it shines through no matter what I wear. My allure isn't measured in the price of my attire, but in the strength and grace I carry within. Dressed in self-love and poise, I feel irresistibly attractive, embodying elegance in every step I take.

Every challenge I face is an opportunity for growth and transformation. I embrace adversity as a stepping stone to my highest potential, knowing that I emerge stronger and wiser from each experience. My resilience is boundless, and I welcome life's lessons with an open heart.

I possess the wisdom and insight to navigate life's complexities. My experiences have equipped me with a deep understanding and empathy, making me a guiding light for others.

· ♥ · ♥ · ♥ · ♥ · ♥ ·

I am a radiant force of resilience, capable of overcoming any challenge life presents. My strength, wisdom, and compassion shine brightly, illuminating the path for others to follow.

· ♥ · ♥ · ♥ · ♥ · ♥

I trust in my intuition and inner wisdom, knowing that I possess the courage to navigate life's twists and turns. I am a warrior of love, resilience, and self-compassion.

I am proud to embrace the power of sisterhood and celebrate the incredible bond between my bestie and me. As a woman, I am unstoppable, and our friendship is a testament to the beauty of female connections.

In the symphony of life, my voice matters. I speak my truth with clarity and conviction, knowing that my words have the power to inspire and make a difference.

I celebrate my uniqueness and recognize the beauty in my imperfections. They are the stars in my night sky, shining brightly and reminding me of my extraordinary individuality.

I embrace my body in all its unique beauty, cherishing its every curve and edge with love and gratitude. My body is a magnificent vessel that carries me through life's journey, deserving of care and admiration. In every reflection, I see strength, grace, and beauty, celebrating the wonderful form that is uniquely mine.

·♥·♥·♥·♥·♥·

I am surrounded by an abundance of love and support. I attract positive relationships that nurture my spirit and propel me towards my highest potential.

I am a source of inspiration and support for those around me, uplifting and empowering others on their journeys. My words and actions create a positive impact, igniting the flames of hope and motivation in the hearts of those I touch. Together, we rise and thrive, creating a world filled with love and possibility

I take pride in the success of my fellow women, for their achievements are a testament to our collective strength. By supporting and uplifting each other, gently adjusting each other's crowns rather than competing, we create a powerful sisterhood. Together, we rise, our collective power outshining any challenge we face

I celebrate my uniqueness and recognize the beauty in my imperfections. They are the stars in my night sky, shining brightly and reminding me of my extraordinary individuality.

I confidently step into my power, making choices that align with my values and aspirations. My potential is limitless, and every day I move closer to achieving my dreams. I trust in my journey, knowing that I am exactly where I need to be.

I deeply value and respect myself, setting healthy boundaries that protect my well-being and allow me to thrive in all aspects of life. By setting healthy boundaries that prioritize my well-being, I create a strong foundation for personal growth and inner harmony.

I am a fierce advocate for myself and all women, championing equality, justice, and unity. I pledge to not judge other women but instead embrace and accept each other's unique journeys and experiences, supporting each other's growth and aspirations. Together, we rise, creating a future where every woman's potential knows no bounds.

www.ingramcontent.com/pod-product-compliance
Lightning Source LLC
Chambersburg PA
CBHW081005120626
46546CB00010B/3025